M000216160

Newcomers Arrive

Harcourt

SCHOOL PUBLISHERS

Visit *The Learning Site!* www.harcourtschool.com

Exploration and Technology

READ TO FIND OUT **Why did Europeans look for a sea route to Asia?**

By the 1400s, Europeans were going to China to trade. The trip by land was long and hard. But they did not know of a way to go by sea. They did not have the **technology**, or scientific knowledge, for such a trip.

In time, Europeans learned more about **navigation**, or how to follow a route. They began making expeditions in search of a sea route to Asia. An **expedition** is a trip taken with the goal of exploring. They found a way to get to China by sailing south around Africa and then east across the Indian Ocean.

Europeans began exploring in caravels (right). They were smaller and faster than earlier kinds of ships. Christopher Columbus (inset) told the king and queen of Spain

A sailor named Christopher Columbus thought of another way to sail to China. He wanted to sail west across the Atlantic Ocean. The king and queen of Spain agreed to help. Columbus promised them he would find riches and new lands.

Columbus sailed in 1492. After two months, he and his men reached land. Columbus thought they were in India. But they were on an island near what is today the United States.

READING CHECK ☼ **MAIN IDEA AND DETAILS Why did Europeans look for a sea route to Asia?**

Navigational Tools

Background For hundreds of years, sailors used different kinds of tools to explore faraway lands and return home.

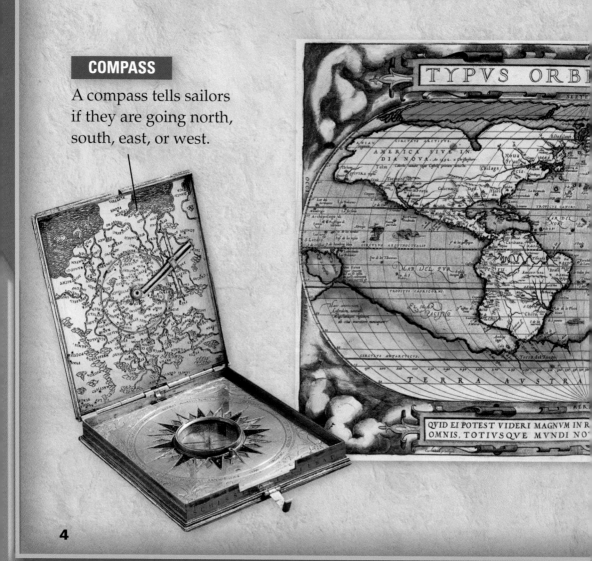

COMPASS

A compass tells sailors if they are going north, south, east, or west.

TYPVS ORBI

AMERICA SIVE IN
DIA NOVA.

MAR DEL ZVR

TERRA AVSTRA

QVID EI POTEST VIDERI MAGNVM IN R
OMNIS, TOTIVSQVE MVNDI NO

CHRONOMETER

A chronometer tells the right time. Sailors used it to find their longitude.

ASTROLABE

Sailors used an astrolabe to find their latitude, based on the heights of the sun and the North Star.

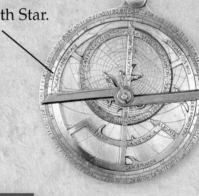

MAP

The compass and other tools helped people make better maps. This map of the world was made in 1574.

1 How might the weather affect the use of the astrolabe?

2 Why would sailors need to keep track of time?

A Changing World

READ TO FIND OUT **What did Europeans find in the Americas?**

After Columbus, others began to cross the Atlantic Ocean. The king of England paid John Cabot to make the trip. The king wanted new lands and riches. In 1497, Cabot landed in what is now Canada. He thought he had reached Asia!

In 1499, Amerigo Vespucci (veh•SPOO•chee) sailed to what is now South America. He found out that this was not Asia. It was a land not known in Europe. Later, this land was called *America* in his honor.

John Cabot landed in what is now Canada.

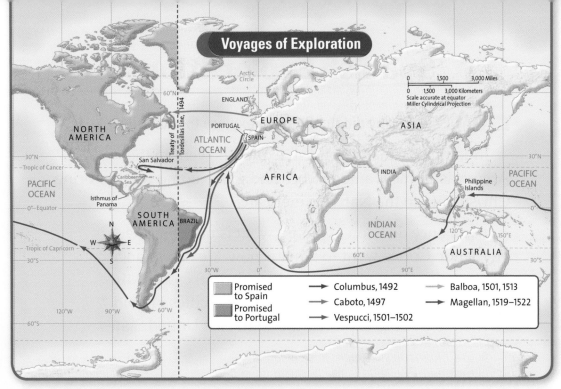

Voyages of Exploration

Voyages of Exploration

ENGLAND

60°N

EUROPE

PORTUGAL

ATLANTIC
OCEAN

SPAIN

NORTH
AMERICA

Treaty of
Tordesillas Line, 1494

ASIA

Arctic
Circle

0   1,500   3,000 Miles
0   1,500   3,000 Kilometers
Scale accurate at equator
Miller Cylindrical Projection

30°N — Tropic of Cancer

San Salvador

Caribbean
Sea

AFRICA

INDIA

PACIFIC
OCEAN

30°N

PACIFIC
OCEAN

Isthmus of
Panama

0°–Equator

SOUTH
AMERICA

BRAZIL

N

W   E

S

Philippine
Islands

120°E   150°E

0°

Tropic of Capricorn

30°S

30°W

0°

INDIAN
OCEAN

60°E

90°E

AUSTRALIA

30°S

120°W   90°W   60°W

60°S

	Promised to Spain	→ Columbus, 1492	→ Balboa, 1501, 1513
	Promised to Portugal	→ Caboto, 1497	→ Magellan, 1519–1522
		→ Vespucci, 1501–1502	

One of Magellan's ships was the first to sail around the world.

In 1513, Vasco Núñez de Balboa (NOON•yays day bahl•BOH•uh) reached the Pacific Ocean. He did this by crossing the **isthmus**, or narrow land, that connects North and South America. In 1519, Ferdinand Magellan sailed across the Atlantic Ocean from Europe. Then he sailed around the tip of South America and into the Pacific Ocean. From there, he sailed on to Asia.

READING CHECK **SUMMARIZE** **What did Europeans find in the Americas?**

Spanish Explorations

READ TO FIND OUT **Why did the Spanish explore the Americas?**

In the 1500s, many Spanish explorers went to the Americas. Some wanted riches and glory. Some went to bring Christianity to the Native Americans.

Juan Ponce de León explored what is now Florida. Hernando Cortés went to what is now Mexico. Francisco Vásquez de Coronado (kawr•oh•NAH•doh) crossed the southwest United States. He looked for "cities of gold." Hernando de Soto explored the southeast United States.

At that time, Catholic rulers in Europe wanted new followers. They also wanted wealth for the Church. They believed they would find both in the Americas. They sent religious teachers, or **missionaries**, to the new lands. Some Native Americans held on to their own beliefs. Others were forced to become Catholics.

READING CHECK ☼ **MAIN IDEA AND DETAILS Why did the Spanish explore the Americas?**

Spanish soldiers and missionaries in the Americas

9

Other Nations Explore

READ TO FIND OUT Why did other Europeans go to North America?

In the 1500s, people in Europe believed there was a way to sail through or around North America. They called this water route the **Northwest Passage**. The first country to find this waterway would have an important trade route between Europe and Asia. It would become rich and powerful.

The king of France sent Giovanni da Verrazano to find the Northwest Passage. Verrazano tried three times. Later, Jacques Cartier (ZHAHK kar•TYAY) looked for it. He did not find it, either. But he claimed great areas of land in what is now Canada for France.

Jacques Cartier explored the St. Lawrence River in search of the Northwest Passage.

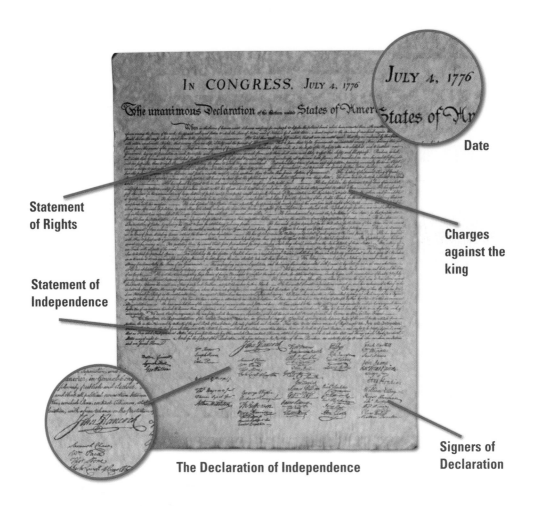

Date

Statement
of Rights

Charges
against the
king

Statement of
Independence

Signers of
Declaration

The Declaration of Independence

On July 4, 1776, the leaders of the 13 colonies agreed to accept the Declaration of Independence. The colonies were now states in the United States of America.

The new country needed a plan for getting the former colonies to work together. The first plan was called the Articles of Confederation. In this government, people voted for leaders in their own states. These state leaders then chose representatives to a congress that made laws for all the states. Each state had one vote in the congress.

READING CHECK **SUMMARIZE How did the colonists declare their independence from Britain?**

AMERICANS AND THE REVOLUTION

READ TO FIND OUT How did the American Revolution affect people in the colonies?

The colonists who wanted independence were called **Patriots**. But not all colonists wanted independence. Some supported the British king. They were called **Loyalists**. Still others took no side at all. Everyone, however, faced hard times during the war. Some colonists' homes and farms were destroyed. Often there was not enough food and other supplies. This caused the price of many goods to rise.

British soldiers burn a colonist's home

African Americans fighting in the American Revolution

Women had important jobs during the war. Some women ran their family's farms and businesses. They cooked food and washed clothes for the soldiers. A few even joined the men in battle.

African Americans, too, helped during the war. Both the Patriots and the British promised freedom to some African Americans who would fight for them.

READING CHECK (Focus Skill) **CAUSE AND EFFECT How did the revolution affect people in the colonies?**

FIGHTING FOR INDEPENDENCE

READ TO FIND OUT **What gave Americans hope of winning the revolution?**

At first, the Continental Army had a hard time fighting the British Army. The British Army was one of the most powerful armies in the world.

The Continental Army, on the other hand, was small. Its soldiers had very little training. The British easily defeated the Americans in several early battles.

General Washington and American troops at Valley Forge

To pay for their trip to Virginia, some colonists worked there for no pay. They had to work four to seven years. In 1619, the first African people were brought to Jamestown to work. Later, more Africans were brought as slaves.

The settlers in Jamestown set up a **legislature**. This is a part of government that makes laws. Men with property could vote to put people in the legislature.

Some Native Americans fought to save their lands from the settlers. The fighting lasted for many years.

READING CHECK ☙ **MAIN IDEA AND DETAILS Why did English settlers come to North America?**

Africans arrive in Jamestown.

15

Pocahontas

Pocahontas was the daughter of a Native American chief. Her name means "playful one." She was twelve years old in 1607, when the Jamestown colony was started.

In that year, Native Americans captured John Smith. He was Jamestown's leader. Pocahontas kept him safe.

Pocahontas was friendly to the English settlers. At first, she brought peace between the settlers and her people.

Time

1595

Born

1607
Pocahontas meets English settlers

1613
Pocahontas is captured by the English

1614
Pocahontas marries John Rolfe

The peace did not last long. In 1613, an English settler captured Pocahontas. He thought her father would pay to make her free.

During that time, Pocahontas fell in love with another settler. His name was John Rolfe. They were married in 1614. They had a son named Thomas.

In 1616, Pocahontas and her family went to England. On the way back to Virginia, she became sick and died. She was only 22 years old.

1617

Died

1616
Pocahontas travels
to England

The Plymouth Colony

READ TO FIND OUT **Why did the English settle in New England?**

In 1620, a group of English people sailed for North America. They wanted to live where they would be free to follow their own religion. They were called Pilgrims. A **pilgrim** makes a trip for religious reasons. They landed in an area that the English called New England.

The Pilgrims wanted fair laws for their colony. If more than half the people agreed to a law, everyone would follow it.

The Pilgrims who signed the Mayflower Compact had the right to govern themselves.

Pilgrims and Native Americans share a meal.

The Pilgrims named their colony Plymouth. Their first winter there was very hard. Then the Pilgrims met friendly Native Americans. A man named Tisquantum helped them fish and plant seeds. He also helped them trade with the Native American tribes. Their life got better.

More English people moved to other areas of New England. They were not friendly to the Native Americans. The Native Americans lost land to the new settlers. This made the Native American groups fight over places to hunt.

READING CHECK ○ **MAIN IDEA AND DETAILS Why did the English settle in New England?**

The French and the Dutch

READ TO FIND OUT Why did the French and the Dutch start colonies in North America?

The French claimed land in what is now Canada. The French hoped colonies there would make them more powerful. French missionaries wanted to bring the Catholic religion to the Native Americans. French merchants wanted to trade with the Native Americans for furs.

The Dutch wanted to trade for furs, too. Their colony was in the New York area. Their town, New Amsterdam, grew fast.

New Amsterdam, 1640s

European settlers fought over the fur trade. Native Americans took sides. The Huron tribe became an **ally**, or partner, of the French. The Iroquois fought for the Dutch and English.

In 1673, Native Americans helped the French find the Mississippi River. Later, another French group explored the whole river. The group's leader said the land the explorers saw belonged to King Louis of France. He called it Louisiana.

READING CHECK DRAW CONCLUSIONS **Why did the French and the Dutch set up colonies in North America?**

Activity 1

Write the term or terms from the list that correctly complete each sentence.

navigation	colony	Northwest Passage
expedition	missions	
isthmus	legislature	ally
missionaries	pilgrims	

1. _____tools helped explorers find their way.

2. A _____could make a country rich and powerful.

3. The _____ passed laws for the colony.

4. Some Native Americans moved to _____, where they were taught about Christianity.

5. The English needed an _____ in the war.

6. Coronado led an _____ across the southwestern United States.

7. A narrow _____connects South America and North America.

8. Many explorers tried to find the _____ across North America.

9. The _____ made a journey to a new land so that they could worship freely.

10. _____ taught Native Americans about the Catholic religion.

Activity 2

Look at the list of vocabulary words. Categorize the vocabulary words in a chart like the one below. Then use a glossary or dictionary to learn the definitions of the words that sound familiar or that you do not know.

technology   demand   indentured   plantation
navigation   supply   servant   slavery
expedition   isthmus   royal colony   borderlands
empire   treaty   self-   mission
entrepreneur   grant   government   hacienda
cost   conquistador   ally   profit
benefit   reform   presidio   legislature
Reconquista   Reformation   Counter-   pilgrim
raw material   mutiny   Reformation   majority
cash crop   missionary   Northwest   rule
represent   stock   Passage   proprietary
compact   colony   colony

		I Know	Sounds Familiar	Don't Know
○	isthmus			✓
	pilgrim		✓	
	colony	✓		

Main Idea and Details Why did Europeans want a sea route to Asia?

Vocabulary

1. How did **navigation** tools like the compass help the early explorers?

Recall

2. Why did Spain set up missions in the Americas?
3. How did Native Americans help the Pilgrims in New England?
4. Why did Catholic leaders think the Americas were important to the Church?

Critical Thinking

5. Why did Native Americans sometimes fight against the European settlers?

Activity

Write a Letter Imagine that you and your family came from Europe to settle in New England. Write a letter to a friend in Europe. Tell your friend about your new life, including how Native Americans helped you and the other colonists.